RESIN JEWELLERY

CRAFTING

HANDBOOK

ULTIMATE Beginner's Guide to Resin Jewelry Making

ADRIENNE ERSKINE

Table of Contents

CHAPTER ONE

Resin Jewellery Crafting

Making Jewelry from Resin

Find out how to make resin jewelry with this step-by-step guide. To make epoxy pendants, necklaces, earrings, and other types of resin jewelry with open bezels, you'll need the right jewelry molds and different techniques.

Beginner's Guide to Resin Jewelry Making

We recommend making your own jewelry out of a resin craft project because it is both fun to make and a statement piece to wear. Resin jewelry that reflects your personal style can be made by you. After you've made jewelry for yourself, consider making a few extra pieces to give as presents to loved ones.

Using this resin tutorial, you'll learn how to make a variety of resin jewelry, from pendants and earrings to rings and necklaces, as well as how to incorporate flowers into resin designs. What techniques for resin jewelry have you been most looking forward to learning?

Into Resin has partnered with us to bring you this post. I only recommend products that I genuinely believe in and believe in wholeheartedly. Please thank the brands that help make this site possible.

In order to create resin jewelry, what materials are required?

The following is a comprehensive list of everything you'll need to make resin jewelry at home.

It doesn't matter if you're a seasoned resin artist or just getting started with epoxy art, having the right supplies is essential.

Molds for Making Jewelry from Resin

A wide selection of resin jewelry molds can be found at IntoResin. Here you'll find a wide variety of jewelry from rings to pendants to charms. With so many molds to choose from, it's easy to create one-of-a-kind epoxy jewelry.

The silicone used in their resin molds is soft and long-lasting, resulting in beautiful resin pieces. The mold is still in excellent condition after hundreds of jewelry pieces have been poured from it.

As a bonus, the resin pieces come out with a glossy finish, so you don't need to polish or sand them.

Jewelry molds to experiment with include:

• 3 Pendant Molds in a Set (great for necklaces, earrings, and keychains)

- Pendant Mold Inspired by the Ocean

- Earring Molding

- Molds for Rhombus Earrings

- Jewelry Mold for Gemstones

Mould With A Spherical Form (for pedant ornaments)

- Teardrop Earrings.

- Lace Jewelry

Pendants with Symbols of the Zodiac

Bezels that are open (I'll show you how to craft with those later on, so stay tuned)

a set of resin jewelry

There are so many wonderful molds to choose from that it can be a bit overwhelming. If you're new to resin art, I highly recommend these two kits, which include everything you need to make resin art jewelry.

Pedant drill, pipettes, stirrers, hook screws, and a resin jewelry kit are all included in this kit. 2 pendant epoxy molds, gemstone pendant molds, a charm bracelet mold and 2 adorable bear molds are all included in the kit.

Mold for jewelry casting has over 40 different shapes and sizes. It's the ideal mold for casting a wide range of necklaces and other accessories.

CHAPTER TWO

Jewelry Making Resin of Choice

The quality of the epoxy resin you use when making epoxy resin jewelry is of the utmost importance. For this resin jewelry tutorial, I used my all-time favorite epoxy resin: IntoResin's Fast Cure Casting Resin.

Since I've been using it, I've developed a strong appreciation for the high standard of the product. Here are some things you should know:

Resin and hardener are mixed in a 1:1 ratio, and the product's volume is recorded.

Hardener must be stirred in for 5 minutes before the resin and hardener can be mixed together. After putting the resin and hardener together, you have about 20 minutes of working time.

It takes between 8 and 12 hours to cure. Casting resins that require 24 to 48 hours of curing are a stark contrast.

After pouring, most bubbles rise to the surface and dissipate. • Almost bubble-free: I didn't find it necessary to use a lighter or heat gun to dissolve bubbles.

Resin cures crystal clear, as evidenced by the photos.

• No yellowing: Using the Fast Cure Casting Resin, I made resin dice and resin ornaments a few months ago. Despite their age, the ornaments and dice are still in mint condition. There's no sign of yellowing whatsoever!

Use the manufacturer's instructions if you're using a different resin.

Placing items in the resin

Almost anything goes when it comes to decorating. Resin jewelry can be dressed up and styled with a variety of colors and materials. Resin can be used to make a variety of things, such as these:

In order to achieve vibrant colors in resin, it is ideal to use resin dyes. The company IntoResin sells an assortment of 15 epoxy dyes in every hue imaginable. In order to preserve the resin's translucent qualities, this colorant is ideal.

When it comes to coloring resin, nothing beats mica powder. Mica colors are available in every shade conceivable. Adds an understated sparkle to the resin and makes it opaque, making it ideal for bright and vibrant colors.

It's a great idea to decorate your handmade resin jewelry with a variety of embellishments such as dried flowers, gold leaf, and rhinestones. I'll show you how to use these materials to make beautiful resin jewelry at home yourself.

Tools

The following materials and tools will be required as soon as your epoxy resin and jewelry molds are ready:

Mixing the resin and hardener in plastic cups is essential.

• Popsicle sticks or wooden stirrers for blending.

When pouring resin rings, precision is key, and disposable plastic pipettes are the best tool for the job.

• Using toothpicks and a fine needle, burst air bubbles and perfect the details.

• Tweezers for inserting dried flowers and ornaments.

Hands are protected from resin exposure with nitrile gloves.

Make sure you don't inhale any resin fumes by wearing a mouth or face mask.

You can protect your work surface from drippings and spills with a drop sheet, wax paper, or a resin mat. It is extremely difficult to remove uncured resin.

It's time to get creative with wearable art. For my resin jewelry, I used a large jewelry epoxy mold and primarily worked with smaller gemstone shapes. Here's a step-by-step breakdown of the procedure:

What do I do first?

It's a good idea to get an idea of your desired aesthetic before you begin. Is your preference for nature-inspired jewelry with dried botanicals or something gold and glittery?

After 25 to 30 minutes, resin begins to soften. You only have a limited amount of time to complete your jewelry design once the resin and hardener have been mixed. Set up your molds, mixing cups, safety goggles, as well as any other supplies you'll need.

The first step is to prepare your workspace.

Keep your workspace free of clutter and dust. Drop sheets or old newspapers can be used to protect your workspace.

• Organize all of your supplies and equipment.

Get nitrile gloves and a mouthpiece.

Step 2: Combine epoxy resin.

• The Fast Cure Casting Resin has a volume ratio of 1 part resin to 1 part. So, draw two measurements lines on two disposable plastic cups. If you're working with a different resin brand, be sure to check the manufacturer's instructions to ensure that you're using the correct amount of resin for your project.

• Divide the resin and hardener equally among the cups.

• Add the hardener to the resin and mix thoroughly.

• Stir for 5 minutes with a wooden spoon. Make sure there are no more streaks visible between the resin and hardener,

CHAPTER THREE

Avoid the formation of air bubbles by stirring the mixture slowly. My preferred method of releasing bubbles is to gently tap the container on the work surface.

Step 3: Add color to resin

• Add a few drops of alcohol ink or mica powder to the resin if desired.

Colorant should be evenly dispersed and all clumps of powder or ink have been broken down.

• I colored one cup of epoxy with light pink mica, and the other with glitter and metal leaf.

Mold the resin

• Next, fill the mold with resin using your pipettes.

• To get a marbled look, I used two pipettes and resin at the same time.

Keep an eye on the little knob at the top of a pendant mold if you're pouring resin into it.

If bubbles appear on the surface, use a toothpick or needle to puncture them. If you use a heat gun to treat the resin, you run the risk of blowing the resin out of the mold.

Step 7: Treat

At room temperature, allow the resin to cure undisturbed.

• IntoResin's Fast Cure Casting resin takes between 8 and 12 hours to cure. If you're using a different brand or type of resin, the curing time may be anywhere from 24 to 48 hours.

Step 8: Take the mold out of the oven.

Removing the resin from the mold after it has dried completely is the next step. To remove the shapes, simply push them out of the mold.

• Tip: Use scissors or a blade knife to trim away any overflow or spills.

Idea For Resin Jewelry

You should have a beautiful collection of resin gems and pendants by now. Your jewelry is now complete and ready to be worn.

When it comes to resin jewelry, there are a variety of ways to apply jewelry hardware.

You'll learn how to make necklaces, earrings, and rings, as well as how to drill holes for pendants. Afterwards, we'll be working with open bezels and resin flowers in jewelry. Isn't it exciting?

Recycled Plastic Necklace

The ornament we just poured can be turned into a simple resin pedant necklace by following these steps:

Start by digging a hole. Drill a hole in the top of an ornament with the small drill that comes with the resin jewelry kit. The tiniest drill bit is the most efficient. Immediately after the resin has cured, perform this step. The resin will still be pliable, making it easier to mold and shape..

Screw the hook in place. Then, insert the screw hook into the resin ornament by twisting it inward. This little pedant can now be attached to a necklace.

Resin earring making instructions

DIY resin earrings that are easy to make at home

Ear studs are an easy way to get started. It's easy to make resin ear studs that are both adorable and functional. Flat pad ear studs are required. The best steel is nickel-free and hypoallergenic.

Pour resin in the first place. Put the resin into the mold first. Earring studs benefit from more compact forms.

a mild remedy Allow the resin to cure for a minimum of four to five hours. The resin's texture should be thick and viscous, but it should not be completely solid.

Insert the study Push a stud into the center of the resin ornament once the resin has hardened and is no longer a liquid state. Earrings that aren't standing straight on the post will look crooked.

4. Finish the healing process. Unmold the mold after it has cured completely. The epoxy resin stud earrings are now complete, with the stud securely attached to the resin.

Earrings with dangles

Pedant resin earrings can be made in one of two ways. Earring hooks with pendants attached are a no-brainer. You can also attach an earring hook to a resin gemstone by drilling a screw hook into it (as you see in the photo on the right).

epoxy rings

If you want to make resin rings that look stunning, you'll need both rings and resin gemstones. But if you prefer, you can use any kind of ring that catches your eye. Steps to follow:

1. Use a glue gun to adhere the paper. Glue the ring to the back of your resin gemstone with a single drop of superglue.

2. Adhere. Press firmly for 30 seconds after putting the pieces together.

3. Dry. For the next 12 to 24 hours, leave the ring alone. The cured adhesive can be cut away if necessary.

CHAPTER FOUR

I also have a resin ring tutorial that includes a step-by-step guide and various design suggestions.

Resin Flower Pendants You Can Make Yourself

What about some resin flower jewelry? I'm making resin jewelry with dried flowers using the pendant mold included in this set. Flowers and leaves that are small enough to fit in the mold will also be necessary. Here's a step-by-step guide to making resin flower jewelry:

Organize the design layout. Consider your resin flower pendant design before you pour the resin. It's fun for me to experiment with different combinations of flowers in the mold until I find one I like. Cut and shorten flowers and leaves to fit the mold if necessary.

Pour the foundation. Using a funnel, pour resin into the mold to the halfway point. Make certain that the resin fills in all of the gaps and wraps around the knob that causes the hole to form.

Add botanicals to the mix. Carefully place your preserved plants in the resin, one by one.

Pedant of the seal. Seal the botanicals in place with a second layer of resin, making sure that no plant material protrudes.

Cure and remove the mold. Remove the epoxy resin pendant from the mold after the resin flower jewelry has had time to cure.

Is it possible to use real flowers in resin?

Casting fresh flowers in resin will not only cause them to wilt and rot, but it may also alter the color of the resin itself. Ensure that your botanicals are completely flat and dry before arranging them in a composition.

Molded Resin

Small metal frames that can be filled with resin are known as bezels. A hole in the metal frame allows you to attach the bezel to jewelry, such as necklaces or earrings, or use it as a key chain charm.

Take a look at these directions for making resin jewelry with open bezels:

1. Prepare. For the bezels, dip the Q-tip in rubbing alcohol and run it through the bezels to remove any dust or oil.

2. Seal. A piece of packing tape is used to secure the back of the bezel. Make sure there are no gaps in the tape and that it is secure.

3. Fill. To begin, seal the bottom of the container with a small amount of resin. I added mica to the resin to give it some color.

Decorate the space. Let the resin harden for an hour. Add

embellishments after the resin has become sticky. Nail art set pieces were used to create this look. Let the wounds heal to their full extent.

5. The seal decoration. To keep the decorations in place, coat the area with a thin layer of clear resin. Remove the tape very carefully after the transparent layer has dried. Rub alcohol can be used to remove any sticky residue from the back.

Resin pendants with a tie-dye effect.

I also made a few tie-dye resin bezel pendants. Half-fill the bezel with transparent resin to accomplish this. Using a toothpick, add a small amount of resin color to the resin. Blend a few additional colors in with the original ones.

THE END